MODELS OF FAITH FOR BOYS

MODELS of Faith for Boys

STORIES AND REFLECTIONS ON Heroes for Life

TONY PICHLER & PAULA RIEDER

TWENTY-THIRD PUBLICATIONS
twentythirdpublications.com

TWENTY-THIRD PUBLICATIONS
One Montauk Avenue, Suite 200
New London, CT 06320
(860) 437-3012 or (800) 321-0411
www.twentythirdpublications.com

Images: ©Shutterstock.com; Pope Francis (pages 28, 30) M.MIGLIORATO/CPP/CIRIC

ISBN: 978-1-62785-525-9
Printed in the U.S.A.

bayard A division of Bayard, Inc.

TABLE OF CONTENTS

God has created you to be a very special person!

Do you believe that? *Really* believe that? But you cannot become that special person on your own. You need the help of other people, and you need the guidance of what are called virtues.

It has been pointed out that a young person needs a minimum of three important people in his or her life to grow up to be a healthy, great adult. Those three people are in addition to your parents. Who are those three or more people for you? A grandparent? An aunt or uncle? A teacher? A coach? These are people you know, respect, and look up to in life. And they know you.

Yet there are people that we can look up to in life whom we do not personally know, and they do not know us. They are our everyday heroes. These heroes may be living or deceased. The thing about these heroes is that there is something in their life that we can use as an example for our own life. Each person in this book is lifted up as a hero for you to consider. And each person is linked to a virtue.

What is a virtue? A virtue is a standard by which we live. It is the ability to act on that standard and to live up to it. There are many virtues. Which virtues do you most hold up and follow in your life? With what hero or heroes do you most identify?

Each chapter focuses on a different everyday hero. The life of the person is discussed. Then the virtue that most fits his or her life is described. An activity is provided for you to work with the virtue. A reflection question or two is also provided to help you think about how the virtue is lived out in your own life. Finally, an action step is included to help you in living out the virtue and following in the footsteps of the everyday hero.

What hero do you most identify with in your life? Maybe one day someone will say that it is *you* who they want to be like! Be a hero!

Mahatma Gandhi

I proved that our gifts and talents are not always known to us early in life. I was born in India in 1869. I was trained as a lawyer and was the first to use nonviolent civil disobedience in a dispute in South Africa—the country where I was working. Shortly thereafter, I returned to my native India to organize peasants and farmers to protest against discrimination and high taxes. I led the people in nonviolently fighting for self-rule, as opposed to being governed by England.

I was imprisoned many times and endured long periods of fasting from food and drink as a way to protest the abuses of the time. But it all paid off as India was granted independence from Great Britain in 1947. I was assassinated by a gunman on January 30, 1948.

His Virtue

FAITH

"I have faith in you!" "Oh, ye of little faith!" "Have a little faith in me." Have you ever heard these sayings? Maybe they were said of you. Maybe you used them when speaking of someone else. Whichever, faith is the virtue that requires a little leap. Sometimes a big leap! Faith is a gift from God that helps you take that leap from what you can see and touch to what you cannot see and cannot touch.

ACTIVITY

Faith Labyrinth: A labyrinth is a sacred path. Find your way from the start point to the center of the labyrinth, reflecting on the faith of Mahatma Gandhi as he stood up for his people by fasting and prayer.

JOURNAL / REFLECTION

Has faith ever given you the courage to stand up for something? If so, give an example.

ACTION

While sitting in a public space, take a moment to see life through the eyes of those who surround you.

HIS WORDS

Live as if you were to die tomorrow. Learn as if you were to live forever.

An eye for an eye only ends up making the whole world blind.

We may never be strong enough to be entirely nonviolent in thought, word, and deed. But we must keep nonviolence as our goal and make strong progress towards it.

Amelia Earhart

Do you believe I can fly? I certainly did! I was the first woman to fly solo across the Atlantic Ocean. I was determined to do it and I did! On May 20, 1932, I set out from Newfoundland, Canada, and flew across the ocean to Londonderry, Northern Ireland, where I landed the next day, on May 21. This wasn't my only record for flight, but it was probably the one that most people remember the most.

I was involved in more than just flying airplanes. I also taught at Purdue University and became an early supporter of equal rights for women. One of the things I am most proud of is that I helped to form the Ninety-Nines, an organization that supported female pilots.

In 1937 my navigator and I were attempting to fly around the world when our airplane disappeared in the Pacific Ocean. My navigator and I know what happened, but unfortunately no one else does; so our disappearance remains an unsolved mystery.

Her Virtue

HOPE

It is said that without vision, it is difficult for people to move forward. Another way to speak about vision is with the word *hope*. Hope is when you want or desire something, and you expect that, at least someday, this desire will become a reality. You might hope you will receive a new bike for Christmas. You might even expect to receive one, as you drop hints (maybe even writing a letter to Santa Claus) that the bike you really want can be found in a store at the mall. We do not always have our hopes become reality. But if we lose hope, we lose everything. Keep the flames of hope alive!

Amelia Earhart had a hope that would not die. She hoped that she had the equipment, knowledge, and the energy to fly across the ocean. She hoped that she would make it without crashing and become the first woman to do so. Her hope turned into a reality when she landed in Ireland after the long flight. She hoped that she could do it! And she *did* it!

ACTIVITY

Amelia's flight: Find the words that fit each cloud and help Amelia fly across the ocean: **dream**, **wish**, **faith**, **belief**, **goal**, **promise**.

HER WORDS

You can do anything you decide to do. You can act to change and control your life; and the procedure, the process, is its own reward.

I have often said that the lure of flying is the lure of beauty.

JOURNAL / REFLECTION

What is something you hope for, and how can you make that dream become a reality?

ACTION

Share your dream with someone you trust, and create the steps needed in making the above dream become a reality.

Martin Luther King Jr.

I had a dream! And though I may not have lived long enough to fully realize that dream, I did help to make great strides in the civil rights of African Americans. Beginning in 1955, while serving as a Baptist minister for a church in Montgomery, Alabama, I led the bus boycott that was inspired by Rosa Parks. Then I continued to lead the march toward civil rights until I was killed by an assassin in Memphis, Tennessee, in 1968.

I must admit that one of my favorite and most memorable moments was the March on Washington in 1963. Nearly 250,000 people, both black and white, gathered at the Lincoln Memorial on the Mall in Washington, DC. There I delivered what is still considered one of the greatest speeches of all time—my "I Have a Dream" speech.

I was humbled to receive the Nobel Peace Prize in 1964. I was assassinated in 1968 prior to my involvement in what I called the Poor People's March. Each January people celebrate and remember me on my special day.

His Virtue

LOVE

How many songs do you know that have the word "love" in them? Go ahead! Count them up! We will give you time. OK, are you back? How many did you remember? Why are there so many songs with the word "love"? Probably because love is the foundation of all of our relationships. Think about your relationship with your parents. Or your brother or sister, if you have one. Or your best friend. What do all of these relationships have in common? Most likely, love. You love and you are loved. That is the basis of our relationship with God too. God has loved us so much that God brought us into the world and even sent his only Son, Jesus, to us over 2,000 years ago to show us how to love. Check it out in the Bible. Love is written all over it!

Martin Luther King Jr. was a man of love. He loved his family. He loved his neighbors. And he loved all people—but especially those who shared his skin color. Martin Luther King Jr. loved everyone so much that he fought for the freedom of all African Americans and dreamed of the day when everyone would love each other—black and white, rich and poor, male and female. Like Jesus, Martin Luther King Jr. loved people so much that it eventually cost him his life. How much do you love?

ACTIVITY

Using the list below, unscramble the letters in the hearts.

Care
Emotion
Friendship
Devotion
Charity
Like

dinsfipher

voditone

hiacryt

elki

acer

mootine

HIS WORDS

Darkness cannot drive out darkness; only light can do that. Hate cannot drive out hate; only love can do that.

I have a dream that my four little children will one day live in a nation where they will not be judged by the color of their skin, but by the content of their character.

Faith is taking the first step even when you don't see the whole staircase.

JOURNAL / REFLECTION

What is the person or thing that you love most in life?

ACTION

Ask a family member to tell you about their day.

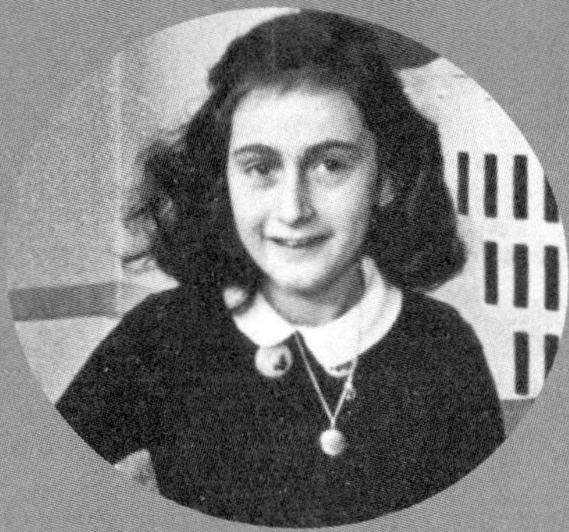

Anne Frank

Have you ever read my book, *The Diary of a Young Girl*? If not, make it a homework assignment! I was a young Jewish girl who grew up in Amsterdam, Netherlands, in the 1930s and '40s. When the Nazis came into power and controlled my home country, my family and I needed to go into hiding, finding a safe place behind a wall in my father's office. While in hiding I kept a journal, or diary, until my family and I were captured by the Nazis and placed in a concentration camp. I was killed in the death camp at the age of fifteen, during the spring of 1944. My diary was discovered by my father's secretary. *The Diary of a Young Girl* has since become a best seller, translated into sixty languages and read by millions.

In June 1999, *Time Magazine* published a special edition called: "Time 100: The Most Important People of the Century." I was honored to be one of those people.

Her Virtue

KINDNESS

Kindness just comes naturally to some people. Especially young girls and boys. It is almost as if they were wired that way. God created you to be good and kind. Check it out in the first chapter of Genesis, the first book of the Bible. Each day God creates something. And at the end of each day God sits back and reflects on the goodness and kindness that has been created. "And God saw that it was good." And the best thing is that we are created in the image and likeness of God, who happens to be all good and all kind. So we have that going for us! We just need to try to live up to that each and every day. Be kind!

Anne Frank was a kind girl. Face it—if you and your family were holed up in a room for hours, day after day would you be kind to each other? Your nerves would be shot. Your family would be tense and scared. How could you be kind to each other? Somehow Anne Frank knew exactly how to do this. She was born in the image and likeness of God, and she showed that every day of the fifteen years of her life. Can we say the same?

ACTIVITY

To open the diary, fill in the missing letters. Then unscramble the letters to use the key in finding the image and likeness of God in you.

How wo__derful it i__ that nobo__y need wait a sin__le m__ment before __tarting to impr__ve th__ world.

__ __ __ __ __ __ __ __

JOURNAL / REFLECTION

Do you see the goodness in others?
How does that help you to be kind?

ACTION

Make something for someone that you know they will appreciate and give it to them.

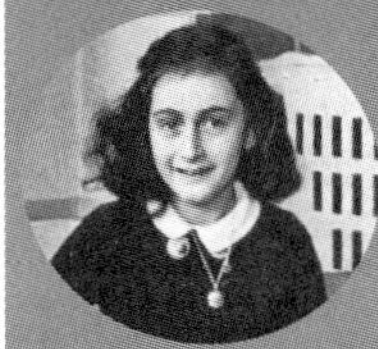

HER WORDS

Everyone has inside of them a piece of good news. The good news is that you don't know how great you can be! How much you can love! What you can accomplish! And what your potential is!

Human greatness does not lie in wealth or power, but in character and goodness. People are just people, and all people have faults and shortcomings, but all of us are born with a basic goodness.

Bill and **Melinda Gates**

People know us as a couple who is worth billions (103 billion at last count). This is Melinda. I was born in Dallas, Texas, in 1964. After being introduced to the Apple II computer as a young woman, I quickly became interested in computer programming. I graduated from Duke University, having earned an undergraduate degree and Master of Business Administration. I then held a position at Microsoft until I married the love of my life—Bill—who happened to own the company.

And this is Bill. I was born in 1955 in Seattle, Washington. After attending Harvard University for two years, I dropped out of school to form, with Paul Allen, Microsoft, a company that became a computer giant. I don't recommend that you take that route, but it did work out for me. I went on to become one of the richest people in the world as the company, and the computer industry in general, really took off in the 1980s and '90s.

Together, we formed the Bill and Melinda Gates Foundation in 2000. The foundation has distributed over 30 billion dollars to charities around the world.

Their Virtue

GENEROSITY

That is one way to look at generosity. We are blessed with so much, especially in the United States. How well do we give away some of our things? John the Baptist tells his followers that if they have two coats they should give away one to the poor. That is generosity. Are you generous? Do you keep everything for yourself or do you give away some of what you have? Give until it hurts.

Bill and Melinda Gates certainly have two coats! They are wealthy people who made a fortune through their work with computers. Rather than keeping their riches all for themselves, Bill and Melinda opened their hearts, and their wallets, to the poor. They are known for their generosity through the Bill and Melinda Gates Foundation. They definitely have shared their second coats!

ACTIVITY

Jesus said, "Sell your possessions and give to the poor and you will have treasure in heaven." **Which one of these dollar bills is not like the others?**

THEIR WORDS

If you are successful, it is because somewhere, sometime, someone gave you a life or an idea that started you in the right direction. Remember also that you are indebted to life until you help some less fortunate person, just as you were helped.
» *Melinda Gates*

If you give people tools, and they use their natural abilities and their curiosity, they will develop things in ways that will surprise you very much beyond what you might have expected.
» *Bill Gates*

JOURNAL / REFLECTION

In the past, how has your generosity made you feel? How has it made a difference in the lives of those with whom you have shared generously?

ACTION

Give something away to your local shelter or thrift shop.

Saint Mother Teresa

People know me as a short but generous woman of God. I was living contentedly as a Sister of Loreto and teaching schoolchildren when God touched my life and called me to serve the poorest of the poor. In 1946 I moved to Calcutta, India, and formed a community of sisters known as the Missionaries of Charity. The sisters and I served the poor who were dying of leprosy and other miserable diseases. I also served in soup kitchens, orphanages, and schools.

It was because of my work in the slums of Calcutta and around the world that I was granted the Nobel Peace Prize. I died on September 5, 1997, and was canonized a saint in 2016 by Pope Francis. I am now known as St. Teresa of Calcutta.

Her Virtue

EMPATHY

Think of a time when someone you love was sad. Were you sad with them? Did you feel their sadness in your own heart? If so, what you were feeling was empathy. When we feel someone else's pain or can identify with their hurt or pain because we have experienced the same thing ourselves—that is empathy.

St. Teresa of Calcutta was known for her empathy among the poorest of the poor in the slums of Calcutta, India. One of her most famous quotes was: "Because we cannot see Christ, we cannot express our love to him, but our neighbors we can always see, and we can do to them what, if we saw him, we would like to do to Christ." With this kind of empathy, St. Teresa felt the pain of the poor and lepers in her city and cared for them. No greater love is there than that!

ACTIVITY

In what ways have you shown empathy to those in your family, school, and community? How could you do so in the future? Complete the chart below:

SETTING	EMPATHY I HAVE SHOWN	ACTION FOR THE FUTURE
Family		
School		
Community		

JOURNAL / REFLECTION

When have you felt the pain or the joy of another person? Write about it.

ACTION

Watch the following YouTube clip: **https://www.youtube.com/watch?v=1Evwgu369Jw**

HER WORDS

Loneliness and the feeling of being unwanted is the most terrible poverty.

We ourselves feel that what we are doing is just a drop in the ocean. But the ocean would be less because of that missing drop.

If you can't feed a hundred people, then feed just one.

Not all of us can do great things. But we can do small things with great love.

Pope Francis

They say that you cannot go home again! Well I did! And I loved every minute of my time there! I was born in Buenos Aires, Argentina, on December 17, 1936. I love my hometown! After some early health issues, I became a Jesuit priest in 1969. I quickly became seen as a leader in the Jesuit religious order, the group of men I lived and prayed with in community. In 1992 I was honored to be named a bishop. In 1998 I became Archbishop of Buenos Aires, my hometown. I was thrilled! I never wanted to leave there and believed that I would serve those beautiful people until my retirement and beyond. But that is not what God had in mind! On March 13, 2013, I was elected by my fellow cardinals as the 266th pope to lead the Roman Catholic Church. I took the name Francis after my model of faith, St. Francis of Assisi. You see, it is good to have a model whose example you can follow!

I find great joy in serving God's people. I hope you see that joy and peace on my face every day!

His Virtue

JOY/HUMOR

Joy and humor go together like peanut butter and chocolate. You could have one without the other, but together they taste so much better! Joy is the peace you have within you when you know who you are, why you are, and what God has created you to do in order to shine God's love in this world. Joy comes from the inside and beams out to everyone we meet. A sense of humor is something you are born with—it is God-given. Some people are born with the ability to make people laugh. Others have the ability to know when something is funny and laugh freely about that part of life.

Pope Francis always seems to have a smile on his face. The joy he experiences on the inside comes from his many years of experience in knowing that he is a child of God and that God has blessed him with incredible gifts. He freely shares this joy with others, many times through his sense of humor. How many times have you seen a frown on the face of Pope Francis? How many times have you seen a smile?

ACTIVITY

Enjoy these knock knock jokes, and then write one of your own in the space below.

Knock knock.
Who's there?
Tank.
Tank who?
You're welcome.

Knock knock.
Who's there?
Spell.
Spell who?
Okay: W-H-O.

Knock knock.
Who's there?
____
____
____

HIS WORDS

We must restore hope to young people, help the old, be open to the future, spread love. Be poor among the poor. We need to include the excluded and preach peace.

Oh, how I would like a Church that is poor and is for the poor.

I see the church as a field hospital after battle. It is useless to ask a seriously injured person if he has high cholesterol and about the level of his blood sugars. You have to heal his wounds. Then we can talk about everything else.

JOURNAL / REFLECTION

What brings you joy? Write about it.

ACTION

Find a way to bring a smile to someone you meet.

Albert Schweitzer

People have said that I was many things to many people. I was a theologian, organist, writer, philosopher, and physician. Yet, I am probably most remembered for two things: my search for the historical, human Jesus to help us balance our views of Jesus and his divinity, and my outreach to the poor of Africa. I loved the people of Africa so deeply that I founded a hospital for the poor in the African country now known as Gabon.

I was honored to receive the Nobel Peace Prize in 1952 for my writing and works of service with the poor.

When you wonder if you should do your homework or study for that test or quiz, remember me as a person who tried to use all of the gifts God gave me. Now it is your turn. Try your hardest to use your gifts and talents!

His Virtue

COMPASSION

Words are great! When you break down a word to understand its meaning, you can learn more about the word. *Compassion* is a great word! You know what passion is. Jesus suffered and was killed on a cross—we call this his "passion." When we say that someone fully puts themselves into a project or a game, they have "passion." The "com" that begins the word means to do something with another person. Other words that use the same "com" are *companion*, *company*, *compete*. We do not do things alone. We feel for each other.

As we walk through life with others we begin to feel their pain and their joy. We have passion with them.

Albert Schweitzer was a companion to many people. With his medical background he was able to suffer with the people he served. The people of Africa suffered much in the twentieth century. They had a caring and compassionate man, Albert Schweitzer, to walk beside them in their suffering.

ACTIVITY

You and Albert Schweitzer are taking a trip across Africa. Along the way you encounter many interesting animals. Name each animal using the key below.

Rhino Zebra Monkey Ostrich
Giraffe Crocodile

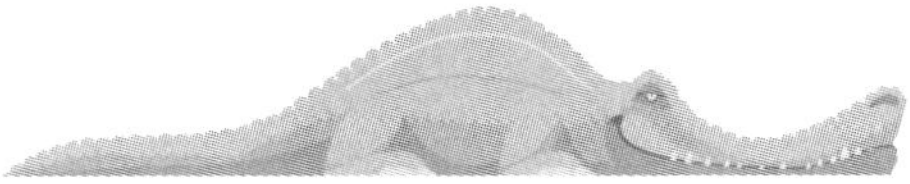

HIS WORDS

At times our own light goes out and is rekindled by a spark from another person. Each of us has cause to think with deep gratitude of those who have lighted the flame within us.

An optimist is a person who sees a green light everywhere, while a pessimist sees only the red stoplight...The truly wise person is color-blind.

Do something for somebody every day for which you do not get paid.

Example is leadership.

JOURNAL / REFLECTION

Who has been a friend to you as you care for others?

ACTION

Create something that will bring a smile to others and share it with them.

Henri Nouwen

Some people have claimed that I was one of the most important spiritual writers of the twentieth century. What I do know is that life was always a struggle, but I hope I contributed something to the world. I was born in the Netherlands in 1932. After becoming a priest and receiving many degrees, I taught at some of the finest universities in the United States, including Notre Dame, Harvard, and Yale. But my life changed forever when I met Jean Vanier, the founder of the L'Arche communities. L'Arche are communities of people, some of whom have developmental disabilities. When I was introduced to L'Arche I fell in love with people whom God created as special.

I lived in a L'Arche community in Toronto, Canada, for the rest of my life. Over the course of my life, I wrote 39 books and hundreds of articles. I died from a heart attack in 1996 at the age of 64.

His Virtue

FRIENDSHIP

That's what friends are for! Think about your best friend. What does that person do for you? What role does that person play in your life? What would you do without him/her? Friends are those who love each other without reservation. They share a love and concern for each other that is not necessarily shared with everyone. Friends share a special bond of trust and respect. You know you have a true friend when that person knows you better than you even know yourself sometimes.

Henri Nouwen was a true friend, especially with those with whom he lived in the L'Arche community. He accepted each person unconditionally. And the most beautiful aspect of his friendships is that most of his friends in the L'Arche community were adults with developmental disabilities.

ACTIVITY

Can you find these words?

KIND
FUNNY
HONEST
CARING
GENEROUS
CHEERFUL
BELIEVABLE
GIVING
EASYGOING
CONSIDERATE

W	T	B	G	I	V	I	N	G	U	V	E
X	S	Q	E	N	W	F	T	D	I	H	A
P	E	X	J	L	L	O	X	T	D	W	S
Y	N	G	Z	J	I	P	G	F	W	X	Y
C	O	N	S	I	D	E	R	A	T	E	G
F	H	Q	G	O	N	T	V	S	M	M	O
L	U	F	R	E	E	H	C	A	G	E	I
F	X	N	R	R	N	L	K	N	B	S	N
E	K	O	N	W	K	K	I	C	Y	L	G
S	U	Y	I	Y	Y	R	N	Y	R	C	E
S	B	Q	X	A	A	V	D	F	Y	R	R
I	X	K	A	C	X	P	F	F	Y	Y	X

JOURNAL / REFLECTION

Who has been a good friend to you? Why?

ACTION

Consider performing a random act of kindness. Some examples might include:

Sit next to a person who is sitting alone in the lunchroom.

Take in your neighbor's garbage cans.

Hold the door open for someone who is walking behind you.

HIS WORDS

The spiritual life is not a life before, after, or beyond our everyday existence. No, the spiritual life can only be real when it is lived in the midst of the pains and joys of the here and now.

Did I offer peace today? Did I bring a smile to someone's face? Did I say words of healing? Did I let go of my anger and resentment? Did I forgive? Did I love? These are the real questions. I must trust that the little bit of love that I sow now will bear many fruits, here in this world and the life to come.

Kurt Warner

It was a long, strange trip to football stardom for me. But I made it, becoming an NFL quarterback and Super Bowl MVP. After graduating from Northern Iowa, I was signed by the Green Bay Packers as an undrafted free agent. But I did not make the team. What a disappointment! Because I was not picked up by any other teams I made a living in a grocery store, bagging groceries.

I just wanted a chance, so I accepted a position with an arena football team, where I became a star. Based on this success, the St. Louis Rams gave me a chance to make their team in 1998. After warming the bench until the 1999 season, I finally became a starter. My career skyrocketed from there: I led my team to two Super Bowls and I won two NFL Most Valuable Player awards. In 2017 I was inducted into the NFL Hall of Fame.

Yet what has helped me stand out as a role model is not only football. My wife, Brenda, and I have devoted many hours to serving others, especially developmentally disabled children. That is what is really important in my life!

His Virtue

HONESTY

Quick! When is a time that you did not tell the truth? How did that hurt another person? How did that hurt yourself? Honesty is about telling the truth—about not lying. But it is more than that. Honesty is doing the right thing always, even when no one is looking. There is an old saying: "What you do in the dark will come to light." An honest person does the right thing in the darkness *and* in the light.

Kurt Warner is just one of those people whom you meet every once in a while who impresses you with his honesty. You can believe him. He tells the truth. Whether bagging groceries to make a living or leading his football team to a Super Bowl championship, Kurt is believable. Can you follow his lead? Let's be honest!

ACTIVITY

Match the football definition on the left with the term on the right.

DEFINITIONS

1. **Calls the plays in the huddle and receives the ball from the center**
2. **The player who snaps the ball to the quarterback**
3. **The player who runs with the football**
4. **When gains 10 or more yards**
5. **The bars through which a football is kicked**
6. **Dashes painted on the field**
7. **Place where fans can get something to eat**
8. **The goal of every offensive team**

TERMS

Running back

Endzone

Quarterback

Goal posts

Hashmarks

Concession Stand

Center

First Down

HIS WORDS

The road to our dreams has many detours.

People are going to forget that I won a Super Bowl, but they're never going to forget the kind of impact you had on them personally.

Faith lives inside of us in every circumstance.

JOURNAL / REFLECTION

When was the last time that you found it difficult to be honest? Write about it.

ACTION

Learn more about your community by reading the newspaper, listening to the news on the radio, and watching the news on your local TV station.

Nelson Mandela

I had a difficult life! But I made the most of my opportunities and second chances. I made the incredible journey from prisoner to president of my country, South Africa. Trained as a lawyer, I fought laws in South Africa that favored white people over blacks. Because of this activity I was arrested and served twenty-seven years until my release from prison in 1990. A short time later, in 1994, I was elected president of the country. I chose not to seek a second term and retired in 1999.

In retirement I worked hard to fight poverty in my country. I also fought hard to eliminate HIV/AIDS, a disease that was rampant in South Africa. I am often mentioned right alongside Martin Luther King Jr. and Mahatma Gandhi as people who fought for civil rights in their countries. I received the Nobel Peace Prize in 1984 for these efforts. I died in 2013.

His Virtue

PERSEVERANCE

How many times have you tried something and failed miserably the first time? Or the second...or the third? Perseverance is the virtue of sticking with it—of trying again when you fail. Remember trying to learn how to ride a bike? Did you make it on the first try? Did you fall? If you fell, did you quit, never to try again? Chances are you picked yourself up (or had someone help you), wiped yourself off, and tried again. You know that old saying: if at first you don't succeed, try, try again!

Nelson Mandela is a model for perseverance. He was imprisoned for twenty-seven years for his work to fight apartheid in South Africa. Can you imagine that? Being in prison for fighting against injustice! But through his perseverance, he was able to keep the faith that he would someday be released. He was able to become a role model for future generations to do the same. Keep trying!

ACTIVITY

Underline the words associated with Nelson Mandela, South African, and prison. Hint: There are ten words or phrases.

ORILFARRESTEDPQNDGTRHIMPRISONED

ZBXDYRNOPTLISENTENCEDPRKMBHJWD

EUWQZTWENTYSEVENYEARSILGPGIFIRU

DIRHNFNELSONMANDELAJGURINHGASM

SOUTHAFRICALGMPERYQIXFAPARTHEID

PZIKGOROITYEWQAPRESIDENTOTJNMW

BMXCHXTRTREISOLATEDQJIJKJBKMBOK

NJLGPDOUDJKLILGPALONEVZCXFGFELG

JOURNAL / REFLECTION

What did it feel like to succeed in something that you struggled with?

ACTION

Have a friend place a blindfold over your eyes. Without your friend's help, try to find your way around the room. Now try it again with the help of your friend.

HIS WORDS

It always seems impossible until it's done.

After one has been in prison, it is the small things that one appreciates: being able to take a walk whenever one wants, going into a shop and buying a newspaper, speaking or choosing to remain silent. The simple act of being able to control one's person.

As long as poverty, injustice and gross inequality persist in our world, none of us can truly rest.

Desmond Tutu

I was the spiritual leader of the movement in South Africa for black civil rights against the system of apartheid. This system held blacks to a lower place and raised whites to power and control of the country. I became Archbishop of Cape Town, South Africa, which was the highest Anglican church position in the country. I was so honored to lead my people in this way. I was the first black person to hold this position. Much like Mahatma Gandhi and Martin Luther King Jr. before me, I stressed nonviolent protests against white rule.

I worked closely with President Nelson Mandela to overcome apartheid. For my efforts, I was awarded the Nobel Peace Prize in 1984.

COURAGE

Have you seen the movie *The Wizard of Oz*? If not, check it out! In the movie, Dorothy, the main character, is a girl from Kansas who has a dream that she meets a scarecrow, a tin man, and a lion on her way to meet the Wizard of Oz. Each character is missing something: the scarecrow is missing a brain, and the tin man is missing a heart. But it is the lion who steals the show. He is missing something even more difficult to pinpoint or name—courage. He is afraid of everything and anything. Is there anything you are afraid of? Can you name it, or is it difficult to do so?

Desmond Tutu displayed great courage. Where did that come from? Where did he get the courage to take on apartheid in South Africa? Probably like the lion in *The Wizard of Oz*, he received the courage to go on from somewhere deep inside of himself. Most people would say he received this courage, not from a wizard, but from God, the source of all courage.

ACTIVITY

Place a checkmark next to the statements that are examples of courage.

- [ ] **Trying a new food that you never tried before**
- [ ] **Trying a new ride at an amusement park**
- [ ] **Standing up for a person who is being bullied**
- [ ] **Completing a chore assigned by your parent**
- [ ] **Joining a classmate in the lunchroom who always sits by himself.**

HIS WORDS

Do your little bit of good where you are; it's those little bits of good put together that overwhelm the world.

God's dream is that you and I and all of us will realize that we are family, that we are made for togetherness, for goodness, and for compassion.

In God's family, there are no outsiders, no enemies.

JOURNAL / REFLECTION

Has trying something new been a challenge to you? Why?

ACTION

Choose one fear you have and pick one positive step in overcoming that fear.

OF RELATED INTEREST

Spirited Lives

20 Stories of Saints and Their Amazing Gifts

CONNIE CLARK

Imagine getting a gift card with no limits, ever. That's kind of what happens at your baptism and confirmation. Except it's not just one gift. You get seven incredible, supernatural gifts from the Holy Spirit.

If you've ever doubted these gifts, or thought they didn't apply to you, meet the people on these pages: Joan couldn't read or write. Matt suffered from addictions. Josephine was a victim of human trafficking. They received the Holy Spirit's gifts just like the rest of us, and they ran with them. Joan led an army, Matt gave up alcohol for good, and Josephine turned her past into a beautiful future. Read their incredible stories—and those of other saints—right here.

Find out how they turned their gifts into action and changed the world. And who knows, maybe you'll change the world too.

64 PAGES | $6.95 | 5½" X 8½" | 9781627850933

TO ORDER CALL 1-800-321-0411
OR VISIT WWW.TWENTYTHIRDPUBLICATIONS.COM

TWENTY-THIRD PUBLICATIONS
A division of Bayard, Inc.